Steven May

David T. Pisarra, Esq.

"What About Wally?"
CO-PARENTING A PET WITH YOUR EX

PETLOVERZ**GUIDES**

LIBERO MEDIA

Copyright © 2011 by PETLOVERZGUIDES, LLC
LIBERO MEDIA
PETLOVERZGUIDES,LLC
1305 Pico Blvd
Santa Monica, CA 90405

ISBN: 978-09831635-3-4

The information contained in this book is designed to give an overview and is not a substitute for meeting with a competent family law attorney who can review the full set of facts in any particular case. No warranty is made, express or implied and neither Libero Media, PetLoverzGuides LLC, Steven May nor David T. Pisarra assume any liability in connection with any use or result from reliance on the information contained in this book.

THE LOVE OF A DOG IS PRICELESS.

This book is written to empower you to know what your legal rights and responsibilities are in relation to a shared pet. Often when people breakup they don't think about how to handle the animals.

"As a pet care provider I have dealt with separation and care for thousands of pets." —Steven May

"As a divorce lawyer I've had to negotiate dog custody. It can be the most emotional part of a breakup for some couples." — David T. Pisarra

Table of Contents

Foreword i1

Our Story
    STEVEN MAY i5
    A Note From Steve's Ex i7
    DAVID T. PISARRA i8
    A Note From David's Ex i9
    A Note About Wally i11

Chapter One
"The Dog Does Not Fly Cargo." 2

Chapter Two
He's Just A Dog! – Not 16

Chapter 3
Do I need a Parenting Plan? 24

Chapter 4
Okay, So just what IS a Parenting Plan? 28

End Of Life Decisions 59

Chapter 5
Proving Ownership and Paying Support 62

    ANIMAL CONTROL 67
    AMERICAN KENNEL CLUB RECORDS 68
    VETERINARIAN RECORDS 69
    MICROCHIP & GEOLOCATOR RECORDS 69
    DOG CUSTODY 71
    DOMESTIC VIOLENCE 72
    PET SUPPORT 74

Table of Contents

Chapter 6

Step Parents and Multiple Dogs 76

    STEP-SIBLINGS 79

    MULTIPLE PETS 80

CONCLUSION 82

APPENDICES 84

APPENDIX 1: RELATIONSHIP ISSUES
    Pets causing conflicts in relationships.......... 85

APPENDIX 2: PET INSURANCE ISSUES 93

APPENDIX 3: PARENTING PLAN 99

APPENDIX 4 – RECORDS..........................108
    MEDICAL RECORDS/12-Month Pet Care Calendar

About the Authors................................111

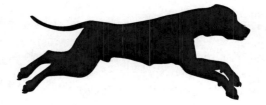

Foreword

This is a book by pet loverz for pet loverz.

For anyone who has ever loved a dog, and lost a relationship, this book is for you. Because not all love relationships work out forever, and with a 70% divorce rate for first time marriages there's no doubt that spouses come and go, but the love of a good dog is forever.

Steven May has been in the pet world for the past 35 years as an expert on training, service to, providing and caring for all types of pets. His years of experience have gone into forming a method to co-parent a dog in a way that allows for the maximum enjoyment of the pet and the least conflict with the ex.

David Pisarra is a divorce lawyer in Santa Monica California who has had dogs, cats, birds and the occasional fish. He has represented hundreds of people over the years and provided solace and solutions to his clients about ways to co-parent pets.

Dogs have been a part of man's family life for

thousands of years now. From the earliest days of the Chinese Dynasties to the indulgent lifestyle of today's pampered pooches, dogs have brought man joy, security, warmth, comfort and have shown us what is best in us, even when we forget it.

A dog is called man's best friend because of their willingness to be subservient. They take abuse and keep loving. They give us hours of laughter and happy licks and ask for nothing in return.

Thousands of words have been said about dogs, but the best may be the idea that they are the opposite of teenagers; a dog is sad when you leave home, and happy when you come back and a teenager is happy when you leave and sad when you return.

Presidents, kings and queens have all spoken of the value of a dog. It was Harry S. Truman who spoke of the need for a dog if you wanted to have a friend in Washington D. C.

From the mythic three headed Cerberus, who

guards the gates to Hades, to the ever resourceful Lassie, dogs have played the role of protector and teacher in cultures throughout time.

Whether as sled dogs, guides, guards, drug sniffers, rescuers, companions, therapists, actors, herders, or protectors, dogs have played a vital role in the development of humanity. We would be a much poorer world but for all that dogs have brought to us.

Today they fulfill many roles, and with greater love and devotion than at any time history. Science has allowed us to learn much from, and about the dog. They help the blind explore the world, and the sighted to see into the souls of man.

A dog can teach a boy how to be a man, and a man how to recapture that boyish glee at being alive. They are the guardians of little girls, and the guides of women to keep the happiness of their youth.

To all the dogs, who have selflessly loved and served, this book is dedicated.

Dedications

This book is dedicated to my daughter Arianna. Her love and compassion for pets has always surprised me at such a young age. Also, for my 10 years of clients who allowed me into their lives to take care of their most precious four-legged furry fami y. For my mother who has been there for me through thick and thin to make my life's passion come true. And finally to a man who mentored me within the veterinary industry, Bob Antin. — Steven May

I dedicate this book to my family who taugnt me that sharing is caring. Their devotion to my success has been unwavering and I will always be grateful for the gifts that I have been given. — David T. Pisarra

Our Story

Steven May

For me separation and divorce was very difficult. Like everyone that goes through this emotional rollercoaster the fear of the unknown was overpowering at times.

One of the nicest things about pets is that they do not judge, take sides or get involved with the process of divorce. Besides dealing with the love in my life, my daughter, and my other love, my pets I found the hardest thing to juggle was my time.

Because my ex and I never argued and have always been extremely civil, the sharing of our extended family was very easy to say the least. Because I moved out, I was only able to take care of one of my three dogs, two cats and one bird. This left quite a daily task for my ex to deal with, plus she had her own emotional dealings and the motherhood of my daughter.

We both understood the necessity of sharing time

Our Story

with our pets. They never suffered the loss of my presence, as I made sure I spent time with them everyday. Once we both decided to sell our home, the tides shifted. It was my time to live with all three dogs and my parrot Tequila. Now I find my ex visiting as much as possible and I am finally able to help in this area while she begins a new life in her new place.

Regardless of our differences throughout our 16 years of marriage, we had our pet priorities in place. Never did we not spend time with them when we wanted to, the veterinary visits alternated, and the love and joy they brings us is still there.

Thank God for Snow, Hymie, Lulu, Winnie, Zowie, Bell Boy and Tequila – we all ove them very much!

— Steven May

Our Story

A Note From Steve's Ex

I have lived with a wonderful menagerie of pets during my marriage and divorce. You may ask, "Who got custody of all your animals after your divorce"? Well, both my ex and I share equal custody of our dogs, cats, and bird. Sounds funny to me that couples argue about such situations. You have to arrange what is best for your pets.

Since our animals are important members of our family, we do our best to keep our separate living situations comfortable and stress free for everyone concerned. We amicably divided the responsibilities as what was best for the pets and our respective landlords. I was unable to care for the dogs or bird because the only pets allowed in my building are cats. I do miss my bird and dogs, but I do arrange play dates to visit and I pet sit when my ex travels. Our daughter now has two homes with several happy pets to care for and play with. I am grateful that my divorce did not affect the way my ex and I treat our fine furry and feathered friends. — Nina May

Our Story

David T. Pisarra

This book would not be possible without the contributions of people like my law partner, Brad Grist. He has been a source of constant support for the past 20 years and I would not have the freedom to pursue my dreams without him. To my writing partner, who encouraged me to work on this book, and who saw the potential in my own life, to share with others and help them in ways that I couldn't see.

My brother Christopher, who raised me from a pup, has been my strongest supporter and I am eternally grateful for your love and dedication. To my high school journalism teacher, Martha Schimbor, from whom I learned much about writing for an audience. To Todd Fraser, whose efforts for the past decade have allowed me to hone my writing skills.

And finally, to Jay and Dudley, for without them, I would not have known the joys of love, the pain of breakup, and satisfaction of reconciliation.

— David T. Pisarra

Our Story

A Note From David's Ex

I grew up with cats. I loved them and their neurotic ways. I'd been around dogs and other animals my whole life, but never actually owned a dog. When my now ex, David, suggested we get a dog, I was excited and anxious! I don't remember any other discussion of breed besides a Dachshund. I was ready. David told me that a Dachshund "will change your life forever."

Little did I know how much my life would change by having Dudley in it. Endless joy and playfulness, tenderness, worry, concern, fascination, and a unique bond that can only exist between man and dog. I finally understood. This bond made the separation of my relationship with David more difficult and painful for sure, but Dudley was a glue for commonality and a source of soothing and healing for us over time. Dudley was and is a dear family member.

Something that's become very clear through real experience is that Dudley is a genuine, feeling,

Our Story

sentient creature. We humans are often guilty of projecting our human feelings on to the animals in our lives, but what I've learned is that through the pain and heartache of a divorce, our pets sense, feel, and often mirror what we are going through. We can find comfort and solace in our pets, and because of that, don't we owe it to them to consider their experience and feelings too? A little empathy goes a long way.

David and I have been able to work out a co-parenting agreement that is often fluid and spontaneous. The key is being as flexible as possible. Dudley has changed my life, and I owe so much to him for being unconditionally warm and accepting. He now has an even bigger family of people who love him, and that gets mirrored back to me, and to us, every single day. Take care of, and be kind to your pets, and they will take care of you.

— Jay Redd

Our Story

A Note About Wally.

Wally is your dog. Throughout this book, when we write of Wally, we mean your dog. Wally is every dog. He is a mutt, and a purebred. A toy, a standard and a tweenie. He is a mix, a blend of the best parts of all wonderful dogs. We chose to use Wally, so that you could picture him, and put your dog in his place.

Chapter One
"The Dog Does Not Fly Cargo."

"One reason a dog can be such a comfort when you're feeling blue is that he doesn't try to find out why." — Author Unknown

In May of 2004 my boyfriend and I decided it was time to take our relationship to the next level, we'd already moved in together, and now it was Puppy Time!

A dog is frequently used by couples to cement a commitment in a way that moving in together doesn't. A dog that two people get together makes them a family of sorts. There's a new love to focus on, and it's a good tool to see parenting styles.

How each of you treats the dog is a very good indicator of how you will each treat an eventual child.

I had always loved dachshunds, the standard size ones. They were tough and durable, while being loving and affectionate.

I located one that I wanted, a 6 month old, short haired, red female. We drove for an hour and half to find this dog. Located way out in the desert, there was a ranch house with kennels. As we walked past the large chicken wire dog runs the packs came alive and barked their welcome.

We rounded the back of the house, and bounding towards us was a long haired blonde dachshund whose coat flew behind her in the wind, looking like a short afghan, she was a beauty. Her owner beamed with pride saying that she was going to be a champion show dog, and even I, being totally ignorant of the show dog world, agreed.

As we came up to the backdoor of the house, and just before we were to go in, there was a birthing pen. This beautiful long haired, black and tan momma had given birth 2 months prior to a litter of gorgeous pups. They were all piled on one another, sleeping their day away. Our host reached down and picked up a little ball of fur, his tiny ears were like velveteen triangles. His face was still all pushed in, his nose had barely begun to emerge to show his true dachshund character.

The lady just hands this soft, and still sleepy ball of

adorableness to my partner, who cradles it to his chest.

I could see the look of sheer wonder and joy in my partner's face. His first puppy. It was an instantaneous bonding of man and dog and I thought to myself, Game Over. We're done here.

We did the obligatory meeting of the dog we had come there for, but I knew we were taking the sleepy puppy home. There was no question that he was coming with us.

Thus began a love affair that continues to this day.

We named him on the long ride back from the desert. Trying out all the standard dog names like Rex and Max. I wanted to name him Weiner and then get a second one called Schnitzel. That was vetoed.

My partner wanted to name him Limo, and get a second one to name Sine. I vetoed that idea. We continued for about an hour with all varieties of strange names, and as we drove down the freeway, I started using the street names as ideas.

Prairie – that was a non-starter. Vega, Molino, Wilson, Curtis, Cypress, all losing names. Then came Dudley Ave.

Dudley.

Dudley Do-Right.

His little head popped up from the towel as he lay in my partner's lap.

Oh. We have a winner.

Dudley it was.

The first night home, Dudley was crying and whimpering. The clock and hot water bottle trick weren't working. My partner was beside himself with the pain of it. I think his separation anxiety was worse than Dudley's.

There was only one thing to do. He slept on the sofa, with Dudley on his chest. That calmed both of them down. The bonding that this brought continues to this day.

Unfortunately, the relationship between my

partner and I didn't continue. We were great friends, but just going in different directions on different planes of being. I'm an outdoorsy guy who likes to go jet skiing, and snow skiing, bike riding and scuba diving. He's an indoor person, being fair-skinned and a redhead, the sun is dangerous to him.

So after a five-year run of living together and building a life, it was time to move on.

Being a divorce lawyer I was determined not to make this a huge battle. I sat down and thought about what I wanted, what he needed, and what was a fair way to divide up the stuff we accumulated over the 5 years together.

There were the usual Christmas decorations, furniture and kitchen stuff. There were pictures and sculptures, and well, a bunch of junk that had no real meaning.

Then there was Dudley.

How to deal with Dudley. He'd been coming

to work with me daily since he was 6 months old. My partner worked 16 hour days, 6 days a week, so really there was no question that Dudley was coming with me.

But he had 2 daddies. Both of us loved Dudley and I didn't want to deny my partner time with Dudley, he just didn't have a lot of it to give.

In my divorce cases I see this a lot. People love their children and then the realities of their lives step in and when they break up, the question is how to maintain the love for, and the relationship to, the children, or in this case, the dog.

So I thought about it. This is what I came up with:

"The dog is coming with me, and you can have as much visitation as you want. The dog does not fly cargo."

That was it. End of discussion.

But then the hard work of making it happen came down. There was the talk about sharing Dudley on the weekends – I gave him every weekend since I had him all week.

There were the overnights; frankly I rather liked having the bed to myself again. It's amazing how disrupting a 35-pound dachshund can be, pushing around a 180-pound man on a bed.

As time wore on, my ex found a new love, in a city 300 miles away. And then he wanted to take Dudley for the weekend. I was fine with it.

But I reminded him that Dudley does not fly cargo. That was a problem at first, but the airlines will allow one dog per cabin if they can fit under the seat. Dudley did – barely.

Sometimes the weekend trips became weeklong trips, and that meant road trips. I was fine with that too.

These longer trips though also meant something else. Out of town veterinary care for the occasional pulled muscle, or upset stomach after finding something truly gross to wolf down.

Dudley has toys. There's Knobby the ball with rubber mushroomy things on it he likes to chase and then grind into the floor, he'll bring it to you to throw and then do it all over again. He's got Hedgie, the squeaky hedgehog toy -- good for thrashing about and to be tossed and to play catch with.

He has his "needs" also. Even though he was neutered as a young pup, some behaviors of boys continue, and that's what Humpy is for. A pillow that has been torn apart by his thrashing and humping and then refilled by me and re-sewn together to continue being Dudley's version of a blow-up doll.

All of these toys along with leashes and halters go with Dudley as he travels. Back and forth we share favorite toys. Some of them we buy duplicates of, like Knobby and Hedgie. And some could not be replicated no matter what – like Humpy.

It's been 5 years of sharing a dog. In that time I've been asked many questions by lots of people about how we do it, and why we do it. The answer is we both love Dudley and, in some ways we still love each other.

Frequently I am asked what are the problems and what are the solutions. Which has led to this book being written. I've been dealing with this subject since my very first case as a young lawyer. I had a couple that was getting divorced after 6 years. They had a home, two pensions, a bunch of stuff, and a dog. There were two things that they fought over.

The first was the bar towels they bought in Ireland on their honeymoon – those little pieces of terrycloth with Harp and Guiness silkscreened on them. And the dog.

The dog was a problem. They didn't have kids to fight over, or to love. So they used the dog. I had no idea how to handle this one, because in law school they don't teach you how to do dog custody and visitation plans.

I had to make it up on the fly. I've been doing that ever since when a couple can't agree on how to handle the dog in a breakup.

Over the years I've had people who wanted to split up multiple dogs – that's not a good idea. Some have wanted to get rid of the dog entirely – I hated them as much as they hated each other. I don't agree with dumping a dog at the pound because you breakup. A dog is a lifetime commitment and you should not walk way from it for frivolous reasons, and if you need to find him a new home, the pound is not it.

I've learned that I can apply many of the same principles that I use for custody and visitation of children, to the topic of how to share a dog. There are differences of course, but to someone who has no children, but loves their dog, it's not that different.

My ex and I still share Dudley. He still flies occasionally – never cargo – and it works well for both of us. We each have the dog we love in our life and in many ways it has helped heal the wounds of a broken heart. By coming together on how to co-parent Dudley, we've learned to see past the hurt, to see what we originally loved in the other, but realize we want different things in life.

But we both want the best for Dudley. Since he brought us together as a family, we're not letting that go.

We just changed how it works.

When Jay married his new husband, there was another dog in the mix. Step-Parents and Step-Siblings happen in blended families and that includes the dogs. With this new relationship for Jay, came a new relationship for Dudley with a beagle. He was used to being the only dog in the house, and now he gets to share his home with a step-sibling. It took a while for them to work out their dominance issues, and to get to know each other, but they did over time.

We hope that this book helps you not only find a path that allows you to share your dog with your ex, but that it helps heal the pain of the broken heart.

Chapter Two
He's Just A Dog! – Not.

"This soldier, I realized, must have had friends at home and in his regiment; yet he lay there deserted by all except his dog. I looked on, unmoved, at battles, which decided the future of nations. Tearless, I had given orders that brought death to thousands. Yet here I was stirred, profoundly stirred, stirred to tears. And by what? By the grief of one dog."

— **Napoleon Bonaparte**, on finding a dog beside the body of his dead master, licking his face and howling, on a moonlit field after a battle. This scene haunted Napoleon until his own death.

Many times when people breakup they treat the dog like he's furniture, as if he is something to be divided along with the plates and plants. One party gets the full use and enjoyment of the item and the other party is denied the use and enjoyment. This works with plates. It's not so appropriate with a dog.

Friends, trying to be helpful in a stressful situation, will say, "He's just a DOG!"

Not so fast.

Just like us, dogs do experience emotional traits. Everyday we interact with them with the belief we can fully understand them and vice-versa. The truth is, dogs that live in a household where a separation or divorce is occurring show signs and symptoms of the stress. They do it by behavioral change.

In many situations when couples argue, yell and are loud, dogs manifest their anxiety and stress by changing their normal behavior. Many times, dogs can become timid, or scared. At other times they become aggressive – like humans they act out their fears by becoming defensive which we see as aggressive. These changes do occur quickly and without notice.

Why do they do this? Because for thousands of years dogs have lived in the wild. Deep in their DNA lies the ability to survive. It is the instinct for survival and the need to feed. Abrupt environmental changes can trigger these behaviors that we think are negative behaviors but if you are not aware of the cause, you cannot fix the underlying problem.

If their daily routine is changed, such as the time of regular morning and evening feedings or when they are walked throughout the day, it will throw off their very finely attuned internal clocks. That causes them to have both physiological and emotional responses that need to be dealt with.

As couples change their regular schedule due to relationship changes it will indirectly, and frequently directly, affect the way dogs live. A dog that is used to getting up for a morning run with his dad at 5 a.m. who is now sleeping in late with mom because dad is not around, can become destructive during the day, because the energy he used to burn off in the morning is still in him, and he wants to do something with it. He may act out by tearing pillows or chewing on a sofa, he can become a barker throughout the day, where he used to sleep through the day.

So when there is a change in overall family dynamic, it will be felt by all the members of the family.

Dogs can make a couple, a family. They are often the third party in a relationship. Ask any new dog owner about their new love and it's all about sleeping patterns, pooping and eating. Sounds just like any new parent with their child.

Sometimes they are what holds a relationship together. Couples stay together "for the children" and sometimes, the dog is the unspoken of child. They forge the common bonds and are where many people test out the commitment of a living together situation before they try marriage or parenthood. Couples may find that they are staying together out of a sense of "obligation" or "it's comfortable but boring" and what's really making it tolerable is the love of the dog.

It sounds crazy, but I've seen it happen. People get into a routine and they stay because it is easier than changing, and they don't know what the future will look like without their spouse or dog.

Once the human is attached to the dog, the dog becomes attached to the human. They become more intuitive and demonstrate their attachment.

They act in ways that seem like compassion. They really demonstrate lovingness and exhibit the desire to bond more than ever. What is happening is your dog senses the sadness; he sees and hears the crying and feels the loneliness and isolation that each party has during the breakup process.

Dogs are remarkably empathetic. It may be that they are simply responding to your new behavior. You may be less playful, so they are less playful. You may be sleeping more, so they are sleeping more. But when you are going through a breakup and your dog comes up to you, and puts their muzzle under your nose, whether it is a conditioned response, or true emotional empathy, either way, it will make you feel loved.

As humans we look for any way to make ourselves feel better. Sometimes we use food, drugs, alcohol, and sex to soothe a broken heart. And sometimes we rely on the bond between human and animal to seek solace. By hugging our dog, or spending more time with them on long walks, we help make ourselves feel better.

When we need the cuddling, the constant companionship and a good shoulder to cry on, the calm support of a dog is a welcome relief. Thank goodness our dogs are there for us.

But as a result of our needy behavior, the dynamics change again for your pets. And at times like this it can be hard on the dog. One pet-parent may be very affectionate while the other is distant and non-caring. This can create a conflict.

Understanding what you and your new-ex-partner are going through is one key element. Having a roadmap of how to handle the dog can help you find your way through this painful process of a breakup.

Dogs teach us lessons all the time. And this is just one more learning opportunity as we seek out a way to move from what was a stable family to a new reality.

Just like dedicating time with children, the same dedication is warranted for pets. And at times it seems more time is needed to make adjustments, as pets do not have the capability to actually communicate with their pet parents.

One of the best ways to reconnect with your dog and tighten the bonds is to do some basic obedience training.

Reviewing the basics of sit, down, stay helps reinforce the pack hierarchy and since dogs like to know their place in the pack, this actually helps calm them down. By asserting yourself as the leader in training you are essentially letting your dog know that it's all going to be okay. You reduce their anxiety by returning to familiar activities.

You have to also let your ex have time with the dog to reconnect. So that they can have their relationship as well. Depending on factors like schedules, age of the dog, how far you and your ex live from each other, and how close they were in the first place, you need to work out a schedule for visitation, if obedience training is going to happen, you need to agree on a trainer, and ideally you should each have the same information at least as to what is taught so that common commands are used.

The point is not to create different commands and behavior expectations with both of you, it is to create a shared experience where each of you has the same command language so that Wally doesn't get confused. When he gets confused, it will only lead to frustration for you and him.

Chapter 3
Do I need a Parenting Plan?

"If your imagination leads you to understand how quickly people grant your requests when those requests appeal to their self-interest, you can have practically anything you go after."

— **Napoleon Hill** (1883-1970) American speaker and motivational writer.

Yes, because if the two of you could communicate well, you'd probably still be together. There's a reason you and your ex, are no longer together. Most likely it is a lack of communication skills on one or both, of your parts.

Communication is difficult for everyone. It's hard to understand what the other person is truly saying, because we often have motivations that live below what we think is going on. Hearing the "meta-message" of what someone is saying is the key that all communication specialists teach.

In mediation training the teacher demonstrates how to 'surface the issue' in a way that allows for a real resolution. This means getting to what each party is really concerned about.

For example, we had a case where one person was arguing about the need to have strong, high quality leash D-rings. The other party was thinking this is an absurd thing to argue over. It's a $10 item why would you spend any time at all fighting over new leashes?

But as we dig deeper, we find that the couple had bought woven fiber leashes, and their dog, an American Bulldog was big puller. This dog had a history of lunging, and one time she was walking the dog, and he lunged, the D-ring broke and the dog got into a scuffle, so he had a history with the Animal Control. Another incident could cause major problems. He would be aggressive and lunge so having a strong and durable leash with a strong D-ring was very important because it was a safety issue.

She was scared it was going to happen again and wanted to make sure it didn't. For her it was more than a safety and security issue. It wasn't really about the leash, it was about the larger implications if something happened. Animal Control could put him down and she wanted to prevent that from happening.

The other reason why Parenting Plans are important

is because they create a working document that you can both rely on for answers. By having a pre-arranged plan, you can both make future plans about when you are going to have your dog, and what you need to do to while traveling with him, or how you are going to treat his medical conditions, and deal with issues such as his nutrition and exercise levels.

These are all areas that can be dealt with in advance, and that takes the conflict away so you can truly enjoy the dog.

Chapter 4
Okay, So just what *IS* a Parenting Plan?

"It pays to plan ahead.
It wasn't raining when Noah built the Ark."
— Anonymous

Parenting Plans are agreements on the subjects of interest to the parents. Every parenting plan has variations in it, but generally most plans deal with the basic issues of who has the dog on what nights, what is allowed behavior, medical care etc.

When beginning to develop a Parenting Plan, it is important to remember to look at the following areas and think about what is going to work realistically. Not every couple is going to have the same issues, or be able to agree in the same manner.

Some couples continue to have keys to each other's apartments to make the handoffs and pick-ups of Wally easier. My ex and I have keys so that we can do convenient and easy tradeoffs of Dudley. It just makes it much easier for us to pick up toys, leashes, and medicines. Other couples would never dream of allowing that level of freedom to their ex.

Everyone must find his or her own comfort level. Generally it is considered a good practice to a brief update on what's going on with Wally. It helps him feel comfortable in those first few handoffs to know the delivering parent is not abandoning him. But you may want to keep the contact limited to talking just about Wally, and not engaging on the other relationship issues, if the breakup is still fresh.

When we draft Parenting Plans we take into consideration the following areas:

- *Regular schedule*
- *Vacation Schedule*
- *Holiday Schedule*
- *Travel Arrangements*
- *Doggie Daycare*
- *Boarding*

- *Agreements on food*
- *Grooming*
- *Veterinary treatment*
- *Moving Away*
- *End of Life decisions*

Even though it seems like overkill, these are all areas that will cause people to fight, and if we can get it down on paper, after both parties have had a chance to think about the issues, and negotiate an agreement, it will make life much easier going forward.

Regular schedule

The regular schedule that Wally is on is the everyday life that he leads with both parents. This is the 7-day a week walking schedule and feeding times and amounts. This should be, for the most part, what was established between the three of you, when you were a family.

Odds are you are not going to change your sleep/wake schedule that much from when you were a couple, so therefore, Wally can stay on pretty much the same schedule when it comes to his eating, walking and pooping. This is important for his general health and your peace of mind.

A dog that is on a regular feeding schedule will have a regular pooping schedule, and if you live in an apartment or don't let him go into a backyard on his own, this is a major concern. Elimination is a major point of concern when you have a pet, and you must be aware of what their schedule is if you don't want to have "accidents" – which are not really accidents. Because if a dog is suddenly eliminating at inappropriate times and inappropriate places, it's most likely because of something that is going on with them either emotionally, or their schedule has been tossed upside down.

Both parents need to be aware of what the dog's feeding schedule and pooping schedule is. The easiest way to keep them regular is for Wally's co-parents to be in agreement that he gets X cups of food at this time and this time, and he gets Y number of walks a day.

The other part of a regular schedule is what days each of you will have custody and care of Wally. The most ideal situation is where you have a regular agreement like a "week on, week off." That may work for some people and not others, they may prefer to have longer periods of uninterrupted time with Wally, and switch to an every two weeks or even every other month system.

Those types of systems make it easy to deal with, especially if one party always has the even number months like February, April, June, August, October, and December. The downside of that is they always have Wally for the Big Holidays like Christmas, Chanukkah, New Years Ever.

On the other hand the Odd month parent gets January, March, May, July, September, and November. So they always have New Year's Day, Memorial Day, 4th of July, Labor Day, and Thanksgiving.

Some couples are able to do a month by month trade off, and then switch the next year so they can each have Christmas Memories or shared Thanksgiving stories.

Vacation Schedule

Vacationing with Wally can be an important thing for some people. Dogs love road-trips and if you like to go to the river or the mountains and want to take your dog along for the long hikes or playing with the kids in the lake, it's an important concern.

This is an area that should be discussed so that each party can plan their vacations. When there are out of state trips involved, the more notice the better. Because sometimes if your co-parent is taking Wally to a new area, he may need to have special medications such as heartworm prevention that he might not need at home.

Different parts of America have different parasites and canines need to have preventive care to make sure they don't catch something, and bring it home which could cause a much bigger problem later. No pet parent would be able to forgive themself if they negligently exposed their dog to heartworm and had to put him down, when for a few dollars, the prevention could be had. Traveling with a pet seems like a simple thing to do, but sometimes the most obvious of issues get overlooked, and that is why it helps to have as much notice as possible about where and when a pet is going to travel.

If one parent is taking Wally on a hiking trip and he doesn't normally go on hikes, this should be discussed beforehand because like humans, dogs need to train for endurance events. That means that both parents have to up the exercise or at least a new shared visitation plan may be needed. Also if the planned hike means that Wally will need boots, he needs to break them in and get used to wearing them. This is not so simple for some dogs, and others take right to having hiking boots. Lest you think we're crazy, dogs pads can be sliced open on new rocky paths and by silicate matter in the mountains, those cuts can get infected and lead to systemic diseases and sometimes amputations, so boots can be a necessity.

Holiday Schedule

Everyone has different holidays they love. For some of us, it is that most American of holidays, Thanksgiving, when everyone is welcome to join and indulge. For others it is Memorial day, the traditional start of Summer and throwing the dog in the pool to play lifeguard to the children. Halloween is a big day to dress up Wally and hope he can get his own bag of candy (But don't let him eat it!)

The presence of a dog at the holidays is almost as necessary as the turkey at Thanksgiving or the candy at Halloween. Who doesn't love to see the young kids trying to ride the dog? What holiday would be complete without the dog underfoot as the dinner feast is presented, hoping for a few dropped scraps of turkey.

The easiest way to create a holiday schedule is to go month by month and each co-parent gets it alternating years. We created a holiday schedule that has the major holidays and then each of you can decide which days and in what years you want to have Wally. The holiday schedule is in the back and is designed for easy use.

Travel Arrangements

This is a big area of contention for many people. How Wally travels is very important, planes and automobiles have different dangers and they have different benefits. In the United States only certified service dogs are allowed on Amtrak trains.

Plane Travel

Air travel is very stressful on a dog, and especially if they are traveling in the cargo bay because they are too big to go in the passenger compartment. Cargo travel can be dangerous for dogs, because of the temperature swings that they can be forced to endure. They can go from being very hot on the ground in one state, to extremely cold while flying, and depending on where they land, it could be another whole shock to the system either hot or cold.

Airlines have strict regulations to follow, both internally and under federal law. The Federal Transportation Agency has issued rules and regulations, which must be followed, but that doesn't mean mistakes don't happen.

We strongly discourage air travel that involves flying by cargo. If you have a large dog that has to fly, we suggest that you look into either a private flight, it's not as expensive as you may think, there are many flight schools and they may do a training session and transport your dog for a fee.

There are companies that specialize in transporting pets and the extra care they provide can't be matched by a traditional airline that is focused on people.

Roadtripping

All dogs love to be in the car, but they need to be IN THE CAR. This is no place to be having Wally travel in a carrier that is roped to the roof. Even allowing a dog to travel in the back of a pickup truck, as romantic and all-American as it looks, is a dangerous place for him to be unless he's properly secured. Even with proper restraints, the openness of the bed of a pickup truck can lead to dangers. Rocks can fly up from the roadway and hit him, he may decide when you are at a stop to go chase a Bichon Frise that is walking by and out he jumps into traffic.

When you are traveling with your dog, it is highly recommended that he have a secured restraint in the backseat of the car.

The standard warnings about not leaving a dog in a hot car are always good to remember. We all know that cars are ovens in summer, and that simply cracking the window an inch is not sufficient to keep a car, and a dog inside, cool. In California it is now illegal to leave a dog in the car in conditions where it can overheat. The owner can be subject to a fine, and in dire cases jail for animal cruelty. So besides exercising good judgment for the care and health of Wally, you should be aware that you have a legal obligation to make sure he is not in danger, each state can have different standards on what is animal cruelty, so it's wise to check it out before you travel.

When working out the agreements on what is allowed when traveling by car, it helps to remember what the point of the trip is, and if the dog needs to be prepared beforehand. If the trip is to go on a multi-day hike, lots of exercise beforehand may be needed for a dog that is primarily in an apartment. Hiking can also be very hard on their pads, and if they need to have hiking boots, a good tip is to have them get used to wearing them for at least a month before the trip, but that will involve BOTH parents working together to have Wally use the boots on each of his daily walks before the trip.

Doggie Daycare

Pet Parents have to talk about the issue of daycare, and what it means to their individual lives. Daycare seems like an easy solution to keeping a dog properly exercised and socialized, but there are risks and costs associated with it, and there are medical requirements. Having a daycare provider who walks the dog twice a day is one thing if it's the teenager next door, and there is a whole other set of concerns if it is a professional service.

The kid next door may have a key to your house and if you've known him since he was in diapers it is one thing, but if it is an adult that you haven't known for a long time, letting them have access to your home is a scary proposition.

Dog walking services need to have some type of bonding and background check before you let Wally just go with them. They should be properly licensed and they should have a good reputation in the neighborhood.

Doggie Daycare is a new category of service that is available. This environment is more like a social camp for dogs to go and play all day with other dogs and be attended to for regular, safe exercise. The providers generally also offer services like grooming and training.

Here again they need to be properly licensed and have a good reputation for how they treat the guests.

When co-parents are looking at the various options for daycare, they need to be aware of the costs and the benefits, but also the risks. Sending a dog to daycare means that for a period of the day, he will be surrounded by other dogs, this can help him become more socialized and make for a happier, more confident dog. That is one of the reasons for a regular daycare schedule for Wally.

It can be expensive though, and if one party wants Wally to go, and the other can't afford it, there can be a conflict. This conflict can be resolved by the one who wants him in daycare is the one who pays for it. The Pet Parent who can't afford it, may then take Wally more on the weekends to parks and other social environments to help continue with the socialization process.

The thing to remember is that Wally may not need to go every day, perhaps twice a week is enough to get him some extra exercise, and keep the socialization in place. A couple of times a week will be much cheaper than every day, and this may be the place in the negotiations where the parties can agree.

Finally, daycare facilities usually want to make sure that their guests have all their shots up to date. This is another place where the financial inequality can be leveled a bit. One parent may agree to take on the bigger expense of weekly daycare, while the other parent can be responsible for vaccinations and examinations, which don't happen every week.

Everything can be balanced out, it just needs to be discussed.

A Warning About Daycares:

Be very careful when picking a daycare, if they don't ask for your latest vaccination records to make sure your dog is up to date, you should move on to the next daycare, because it means that the other dogs may not be fully vaccinated.

Boarding

Long-term care for Wally, when both co-parents are unavailable is occasionally a necessity. This is not always a fun thing for Wally, as it is an interruption in his regular schedule, maybe he doesn't get as much exercise as usual, he may have different food or fewer treats.

Boarding a dog also means expense, here again is an issue that needs to be discussed and shared. There are inexpensive boarders and very expensive kennels, the co-parents need to have an idea of what they feel is fair amount to spend. The odds are that one will want to spend more than the other and the general rule here is that the one who wants to spend the extra money has to accept that they will not be able to get a contribution from the other party.

Sometimes though rather than a boarding house, the parties will agree that they will hire a dog-sitter to stay at one of the homes, so that it is a familiar environment for Wally. Dog sitters generally charge by the night, and may offer discounts for longer term appointments.

It may be $35 a night for three nights but drop down to $25 a night a weeklong engagement. Having a sleep-over dog-sitter is a great way to make sure that Wally gets the best care, and is treated as close to normal as possible. He stays in a home he's familiar with, eats his regular food, has his regular toys and doesn't have the anxiety of a new environment at the same time as being away from both of his pet parents.

A Warning About Boarding Kennels:

Be very careful when picking a kennel, if they don't ask for your latest vaccination records to make sure your dog is up to date, you should move on to the next daycare, because it means that the other dogs may not be fully vaccinated.

Agreements on food

Food. Food. Food.

It's always on their mind. For all dogs, there is nothing in their world as important as mealtime. It's what causes them to do their doggie happy dance.

But for couples who are having trouble communicating, this may be a major area of conflict. Often there is one parent, or a step-parent, who has a very different view of the needs of Wally.

One parent may be of the opinion that no expense should be spared in Wally's food. Some people go so far as to cook for their pets. Others have the view that a dog is a disposal and composter.

But vets and trainers alike will tell you that no matter what you decide to feed your dog, consistency is the key to a healthy pet. Consistency in the type of food they are given, the amount, and the time.

It is important that both households have the same brand of dog food. There's a very good reason for this, if there is a difference in the food, when Wally goes to the other parent's home the new food will be that much more appealing because it is different. Wally is more likely to overeat, beg for more, and scarf down too much too quickly, and then get sick on your carpets.

By keeping the food the same, you minimize the excitement level of being at the new home, and that keeps him calmer and he's less likely to overeat and get sick. It also is better on his digestive system which has adjusted to one type of food, and that translates into less mess for you to pick up as a responsible pet parent.

Treats

Treats need to be considered the same as the food, they need to be similar, they need to be consistently in small amounts and should be used for basically the same purposes.

Some treats cause gastric distress, especially the pig ears and rawhide bones. Co-parents need to agree on the use of these because it can be a very sore point for one parent to give the dog a rawhide bone, and then turn over Wally to other parent to deal with the upset tummy that results.

Grooming

When it comes to dog grooming there are more options than with children. Dogs can be groomed from the basic summer shave to the Poodle Cut, to the very creative artistry that dog groomers engage in at the dog shows where dogs are made to look like camels, buffaloes and zebras.

Most dogs are given a regular grooming based on their breed standards. Some are maintained along show ready guidelines so that they can be shown at any time, and others are only given a good cleaning once a year when there's some special event.

Couples should decide to keep the dog groomed in a standard way, and agree on who pays based on custody. They can split the costs based on the amount of time that each Parent has Wally, or they can do it based on income levels, or a combination of all of the above.

The biggest issue is not always who pays, so much

as what is an acceptable cut and look. No one wants to pay for something that they disagree with, after all that's why we send food back that we don't like, and a grooming job that you hate, is the same thing.

Generally we recommend people have a set selection of "looks" Wally can have, that way there's less room for conflict. He might have a Winter look and a Summer look if he is a longhaired dog, and the goal with the summer look is to keep his shedding to a minimum and to keep him as cool as possible. If he is an outdoor dog a great deal and the summer weeds get caught in his fur and paws, the short haircut may be necessary to avoid matted hair, burs, and foxtail infections.

Veterinary treatment

Medical care for Wally is an area that is a minefield of conflict for people. The issues of what is acceptable, how far to go with treatment, who pays for it, compliance with medication plans, changes in visitation schedules based on recovery times, are just some of the issues that people need to think about .

What is Acceptable Treatment?

Often times one partner has a greater attachment to Wally and they will want to do everything that can be done to save Wally. The other partner may not be willing to take extreme measures, and wants just palliative care, to keep him comfortable and let nature take its course.

There is also the issue of those people who think that science has all the answers and that with machinery and new drugs, all the illnesses of the world can be beaten. Others think that there are natural remedies that are just as, if not more, effective. From Eastern Medicine to the power of prayer, people have different views of what is good medical care.

Co-parents need to agree on what type of treatment

is acceptable first. They need to be clear on whether it will be traditionally western in approach or include Eastern medicine and Naturopathic or Faith-Based.

Time limits should also be discussed, because if a treatment isn't working, there should be a plan B for what to do, and when to do it. Maybe Eastern medicine is tried as a first line of attack, but after 48 hours if Wally isn't improving he switches to a Western based medical care. Or vice versa.

How to handle it if one person wants the treatment and the other one doesn't, means it is crucial to have these discussions before they are needed so that going into a treatment session each person knows what they are faced with, both emotionally and financially.

How far to go with treatment?

There is no easy or right answer to how far to take treatment. This is as personal as deciding what you want done with you, if you were on life support. It can be complicated because we are making decisions for another living creature, and it lacks the ability to tell us what it wants. So there can be a guilty feeling of doing too much or too little.

For some of us, putting an animal through additional treatments that lead to discomfort, even if they save the life, can be a difficult choice. Pet parents who are not on the same page, can run into significant difficulties, particularly if the one parent who has the dog most of the time doesn't want to do a treatment, but it is the other parent who wants to try everything to keep the animal healthy, or vice versa. These types of situations can resurrect the old wounds of the relationship and remind each other why they broke up.

The general rule that we suggest is the Hippocratic one, "first, do no harm." The hard part is finding a common ground, but if you can agree on what is in Wally's best interests, you may find it easier to reach an agreement.

Who pays for it?

The money issue is always a tough one but here are three ways to go about it:

1: You can agree to divide the bills based on your respective incomes. Parent A makes $50,000 a year and Parent B makes $25,000 a year so A pays twice as much as B. Simple.

2: You can agree to divide the bills based on the amount of time you each have Wally. Parent A has Wally 80% of the time, so they pay 80% of the bill, and Parent B pays 20%.

3: You can agree to divide the bills up to a limit. Parent A will split the bills, by whatever formula you choose, up to a limit of say $1,000 per visit, and then the other parent has to pay it all.

How you handle the money issues are limited

only by your creativity and what you can agree to. It can be a source of friction, but certainly doesn't have to be.

Who's good with medications?

If Wally needs to have medication administered to him on a regular basis, the question becomes who is available to do it consistently, and who will remember to do it consistently. Sometimes this means that a regular visitation schedule needs to be modified during treatment.

Example: Wally goes out and gets hurt while romping with the other dogs, maybe he rips a pad and has sutures and needs an antibiotic regimen that demands he have drugs administered at specific hours of the day. If Parent B is working erratic hours or perhaps is not that consistent about administering drugs, then Wally should stay with Parent A who is more regular in their work and can give the dosages on a regular basis.

Shared Costs

When you share a dog, you have to share the costs. Medical care, toys, training, daycare, kenneling, flea treatments, these are all costs that need to be shared.

They basically fall into two categories, basic expenses, and extraordinary expenses. The basics are the toys, food, new leashes and collars, regular grooming. The extraordinary are the medical treatments, and the legal bills and liability if your dog should bite someone or another dog.

Finding an agreement on expenses, whether basic or extraordinary is crucial to making a Parenting Plan work. The goal is to reduce conflict, not increase it.

The basic expenses are generally handled by the person who has Wally at the time the purchase is made. If you're in the pet store and you get him a new toy, that's really for your enjoyment as well, and the odds are that the toy is staying with you at your place. If you're buying him a new collar and leash set, maybe you want to share that cost, as it is an ongoing expense of having Wally, and you will both use the leash.

A note about this is that some couples prefer to buy everything in twos (or fours or more, depending on the number of dogs you are sharing) so that the equipment is the same in both homes. This goes for food and water bowls as well, the more consistency there is, the more likely the dog is to be comfortable and to not act out in ways like begging for more food, or treat seeking.

Moving Away

It often happens that one party wants to move to a new city or state and take the dog with them. This can make it impossible to continue co-parenting, but not always. If they are not moving too far away, the plan may need to change from alternating each week to having a month on, month off schedule. This type of arrangement would never work with children, but dogs are much more flexible and for some people, it might actually be a better way to handle sharing the love of a dog.

Having the break can be a wonderful vacation for both parties and if they continue with the plan, the dog may enjoy it more as well. If there are roadtrips for the transfer, new smells, and maybe a step-brother or step-sister to play with regularly, these are all reasons why Wally might be happier having two homes.

But if two homes are not an option, then a decision should be made as to who gets to keep Wally. This is a painful time for both people usually, because they know that someone is going to lose out on the dog they love. When trying to figure out what is best for Wally, there are many factors to look at:

➢ Who has the room for him?

➢ Who has the time for him?

- Who will be able take time off for the inevitable medical visits?

- Who has the financial means to take care of him?

- What is the reason for the move?

- Is there a new love and a new family for him to be engaged with?

- How will he be taken care of when each parent is at work?

- Where will he be exercised and is this good for him?

- What types of veterinary care is available in the new city?

- Does that matter?

- If Wally is very healthy it may not, but if he has a ton of problems then it may be a major concern.

END OF LIFE DECISIONS

The saddest day of a Pet Parent's life is having to say goodbye to your companion, pal, hiking partner, bed warmer and snacking partner. No one looks forward to it.

Everyone approaches it differently, and as a consequence it is one of the most hard fought areas for people. Letting go is never easy, and to have to make the decision to let go, and end the life of a beloved pet is a painful experience.

Remembering that the level of pain you feel is directly related to the level of love you experienced, may be helpful, but the tears will come anyways. This is one of the times that you can share with your ex, and hopefully you can support each other through it.

Deciding when to let go, is really up to the two of you if you are both taking care of Wally. This is one of those times where the person who has the most attachment should probably be given the lead on the decisions, but with the caveat that the care and treatment of Wally should be the priority, taken in conjunction with the prognosis and advice of his primary care veterinarian.

Chapter 5

Proving Ownership and Paying Support

"I think dogs are the most amazing creatures: they give unconditional love. For me they are the role model for being alive." — **Gilda Radner**

The domesticated dog has been with man for thousands of years. They hold a sacred place in the lives of many as trusted friends, protectors of the home and flocks and have been trained to serve man in various capacities from sheepherding, to guide dogs. They have helped in the war on drugs as drug seekers, and in calamities like earthquakes they have served as saviors to those trapped. The image of the St. Bernard with a brandy keg on his neck is a classic.

Dogs are used as entertainment in our world, acting in movies (who can forget Ol' Yeller and Benji?) and on TV. Before there was TV, dogs in traveling circuses performed tricks, rode horses and elephants.

In medicine, they have served as test subjects, are used as service animals for emotional and physical disabilities and now are cancer sniffing specialists.

Throughout history the canine has been a loyal companion to millions, from king to peasant. The dog is the most beloved of all domesticated animals and for good reason. They are loyal and true, ever vigilant as guardians of hearth and home and they are the opposite of a teenager – sad when you leave and happy when you come home.

Statues are erected to the loyalty of dogs around the world, the most famous of which may be the statue of Hachiko, in Shibuya Station, Japan. Hachiko went each day for nine years after this masters death to the train station, waiting for his arrival. He is loved as a national treasure and his story is known around the world.

The American President Franklin Delano Roosevelt has a memorial in Washington D.C. that features his dog. Throughout history leaders have used dogs as a way to communicate their humanity. People identify dog lovers as kind and loyal and exuberant.

The Queen of England is known for her love of

Corgis and their gentle nature and loving disposition.

Celebrities use dogs as a way to connect with a wider audience. Paris Hilton uses her teacup Chihuahua and Olympian Greg Louganis has his Great Danes.

Throughout legal history, even though dearly loved and honored, the dog has been considered chattel, something equivalent to a piece of furniture.

There are hundreds of breeds of dogs and even though they have different personalities, they all have their fans. From the Chinese Crested to the family friendly Labrador, dogs become part of the family.

They are often one of the first big commitment experience for couples who are developing a relationship with an eye towards marriage. Gay couples and Non-Gay couples who are working through the steps on building a family will use the responsibilities of a dog as a way to 'test drive' parenting styles and see if the relationship should proceed to the next level.

Courts have historically viewed domesticated animals like inanimate furniture, something that can be exchanged for a like version. One La-Z-Boy® recliner is much like another, but one dog is not like another, at least to its caretaker. Ask anyone who's ever had a dog in their life and they have different personalities, likes, dislikes, behavioral issues and traits.

Pug people will tell you that their dogs are very different from Spaniels, and retriever owners will tell you that they have a much higher energy level than an English Bulldog.

All dogs are not alike, but to the court system they still are. One dog is much like another, unless they have been used commercially or have some value as breeder animal.

To be unique, a dog must have something special about them that is recognized for its worth, such as being a model for a dog food bag, or acting in a movie or commercial. Dogs that are used as working dogs can have a value above the average, but otherwise, a judge is usually not going to view a dog as anything special to be divided in a divorce or breakup.

This is why when someone has a dog fly cargo, and they die in route, courts won't allow a claim for damages of more than a few hundred dollars at best.

The starting point though, in any dispute, whether a lawsuit or just with your soon-to-be-ex, is who owns the dog?

ANIMAL CONTROL

Proving ownership is not difficult, and if you've been a law abiding citizen at least one of you will be listed with the animal control of your city and you can get a printout of the license.

Usually one person registers the dog with the city and picks up the license tag each year along with proving to the Animal Control that the dog is current on its rabies vaccinations and any other required shots. Whoever registers the dog can be considered the dog's owner for litigation purposes, and since you have to prove that you have a legal right to the dog, just like you'd have to prove a legal right to a car, having the license is your best bet. It's the most likely document to be recognized by your court.

AMERICAN KENNEL CLUB RECORDS

One of the benefits of having your dog registered with the American Kennel Club is that you have "papers" for your dog. These can be used to prove that you have the legal right to the dog.

Registering a pure breed dog is a simple matter of filling out an information sheet that shows the dog's family history. Usually these will be given to you if you buy from a legitimate breeder, and once you decide on a name you can submit the papers to the AKC® and have your dog registered for a small fee.

VETERINARIAN RECORDS

When you first brought Wally home, you may have had him for a few days, and then it was time for his first checkup. Every veterinarian nowadays has you fill out the paperwork that shows who the owners are, what the health history is for Wally and who to contact in an emergency.

These forms can be invaluable in a future battle over who owns Wally. Oftentimes both parties in a couple will be listed, and that can be very helpful if you need to prove that you have an interest in Wally and are asking a court to make a decision as to who owns the dog, or to make custody decisions.

Because the papers are filled out at a time when the two of you are hopefully still in love, the odds are that both of you will be on the paperwork.

MICROCHIP & GEOLOCATOR RECORDS

AVID®, HOMEAGAIN®, TAGG®, TOGETHER

TAG®, and a ton of other services are out there to register and track dogs and ownership.

When Dudley was microchipped with an AVID responder, we put both our names down, so that if something happened to him and he was lost, when animal control found him they would wand him and find us. But that dual listing is also very useful to prove that we both have an ownership interest in him. AVID® will send you proof of the registration over the internet and help you keep their database current so that if something does happen to your pet, you will be found.

HomeAgain is "a lost pet's best chance" to be found. This is a membership based internet microchip service and it works similarly to AVID®. They have a registry, and a host of other services to help if your pet gets lost. Membership comes with travel insurance to help offset costs if your pet is found more than 500 miles from home. Being a member at this website, is also a great way to prove your ownership interest in Wally.

TAGG® is a new GPS service that allows Wally to wear a collar that sends out a signal so you can monitor his whereabouts from any computer connected to the internet. By having an account with TAGG® you can use this to prove that you have an ownership interest in Wally.

DOG CUSTODY

Who gets Wally? The basic rule on Dog Custody is that where the dog first lives, is where they are going to stay. This is where many people lose the battle from the get go, if they leave the family home and the dog behind, that's usually where the dog is going to be. That's what most judges will order, if they will even make orders.

Often times when couples break up someone moves in to an apartment, and those often don't allow dogs so the moving parent loses out. But, that doesn't mean they have to give up entirely, there are still many options such as weekend visits, day trips, and roadtrips.

Custody can be determined by agreement of the parties and that is what this book is mostly about, but there is the dreaded court ordered restraining order that can give on person control of Wally.

DOMESTIC VIOLENCE

Domestic Violence is a tragedy. It is painful, shameful, and psychologically damaging to everyone in the household, especially children who are frequently the innocent observers. But it also affects the pets. They suffer also when there is strife in the house. The anger and yelling of a breakup can have serious side effects on the pet's outlook. They can become nervous, anxious and start regressing on housebreaking, the same way that children will do with potty training.

Domestic Violence happens when one person physically attacks another, threatens, harasses, or intentionally disturbs the peace and serenity of the other party.

The true rate of domestic violence is hard to quantify as so many incidents of domestic violence, or spouse on spouse abuse, go unreported. Women under-report for fear of retribution from their attackers and men are chronic under-reporters of being abused, for fear of being mocked and belittled by other men, and ignored by the police.

Everyone deserves to be safe and protected, and anyone who is a victim of domestic violence needs to call the police and get a restraining order.

When you apply for Domestic Violence Restraining Order, some states are starting to include the dog in the protection order. The main reason for this is to prevent the attacker from using abuse against the dog as a way to harass or torment the victim, but it works to give the victim effective custody of the dog.

People who abuse others are likely to abuse animals and that is an unfortunate fact. This is one of the reasons why an abuser should not be allowed to have a pet, and in some jurisdictions people have been restrained by court order from having animals based on their history of abuse.

Once you have established ownership though, you may have to deal with Pet Support and paying for the expenses for the maintenance of Wally.

PET SUPPORT

Pet support is money that is paid to contribute to the expenses necessary for the maintenance and care of a pet. It is based on many factors - the time that the parents share the pet, the income levels of each parent, the age of the pet, the number of pets involved, etc.

Pet support can be decided between the Pet Parents on a very casual basis or it can be a very specific, hard fought battle involving copies of receipts, spreadsheets and calendars and insurance premium payments and co-pays.

Chapter 6
Step Parents and Multiple Dogs

"Dog's lives are too short. Their only fault really."
— Agnes Sligh Turnbull

There are two topics that people get upset over, the "New Partner" and multiple dogs. The new partner can be a source of great pain for some people.

When your ex moves on and has a new love, it can be a reminder of the failure of your relationship. It can be infuriating, especially if you try to compare yourself to the new partner and you can't figure out what they see in them.

This is generally a painful and fruitless endeavor, trying to understand another human beings motives and actions is one of the most difficult and pointless ways to spend your life.

I was very angry at the breakup of my relationship with Jay, until one day we were doing an exchange of Dudley and Jay was telling me about his weekend with his new love. I'll never forget the feeling because it was like a lightswitch was turned on for me.

He was talking about how San Francisco had an

unseasonably sunny day and he and his new boyfriend were getting sunburned. It was at that moment that it all fell into place and I realized that we were just different people going in different directions and that everything that happened in the breakup phase was no longer important or harmful to me.

All my anger dissipated in the blink of an eye when I realized that we were not well suited for each other and his new boyfriend was a much better fit.

I would never have had that moment if it wasn't the weekly exchanges we did of Dudley that caused us to chat. One more time, Dudley was teaching me a lesson, and he didn't even know it.

The relationship that Jay went on to have necessarily effected the care and feeding of Dudley, as he now had a step-dad. I wasn't worried about him being mistreated, because the new beau had a beagle already, which meant that Dudley was soon to have a step-brother.

What the new relationship did though, was make issues like what food was being fed, rise to the top and force us to have a discussion about getting both dogs on the same food.

The problem with this was, there were four households to coordinate. David's, Jay's, the new boyfriends, and his ex's. Because the new boyfriend and his ex shared the beagle, we had to get that dog on the same food in his two homes. It was quite a diplomatic accomplishment to say the least!

Blended families don't just happen on the TV. They happen in real life, and while they are not as neat and tidy as the Brady Bunch, you can make it all work out.

STEP-SIBLINGS

When you have a new partner in the mix, and they have a dog, you have to go through the entire introduction of dogs on neutral territory process and be on alert for awhile when they are first together, the territorial fights can happen when you first bring them into a home that each one consider "theirs."

If you need help with the introduction, seek out a reliable trainer who can assist with the introductions and the transition from a single pet household to a multiple pet home.

MULTIPLE PETS

In families that have multiple dogs, at the breakup it is tempting for the Pet Parents to want to split the dogs up and each take one or two. While this seems like a fair and equitable solution from the viewpoint of the parents, in reality it is not good for anyone. It's not good for the dogs that have bonded and created their Pack. They are already going to go through the stress of the split up, and losing their dog pack members only adds to the stress.

Additionally breaking up the dogs is not good for

the Pet Parents who have each bonded with the dogs and would have to let go of the dogs that are leaving.

In general it is better to work out a system that allows for the dogs to keep their dog pack together and have access to the Pet Parents who love them on a regular basis.

CONCLUSION

We hope that you have found this book to be helpful, it is borne out of the pain of lost love, but if it helps others to reconcile with their exes and allows for more love in this world to be shared, then it is all worth it.

We look forward to bringing you other informative, helpful books to foster the love between human and animal.

We'd love to hear from you by email at our website, or on our Facebook Fan page, stop us at a book signing, or flag us down in a pet store if you see us.

Many happy trails and tails!

APPENDICES

The following two articles appear by courtesy of the authors. We are grateful and thankful for their contributions to our book.

Relationship Issues
By Jonathan Klein

How To Deal With Your Pet Insurance Policy When Separating Or Divorcing
By Embrace Pet Insurance

APPENDIX 1

RELATIONSHIP ISSUES

Pets causing conflicts in relationships.

By Jonathan Klein, Dog Trainer

www.ISaidSit.com, 800-400-TRAIN

What are problem areas where pets cause problems in relationships and what can you do about them?

Just like it is with children, couples may not always see eye to eye on how to best "parent" a pet. And because consistency is so important this can lead to confusion for the dog and arguments for the "parents." Serious problems can arise with inconsistent rules and treatment.

If a couple has made the decision to get a dog I think it's essential to discuss some of the issues that will arise. This gives the couple a chance to find out of they're on the same page in how they'll raise their pet and to also create some rules. For

APPENDIX 1

instance, some people may have a big problem with a dog getting on the bed while their partner may not see this as an issue. So the more "if's" you can discuss in advance the easier it will be when the "if" actually happens and you already know how you intend to respond.

Another problem is attention-seeking behavior based out of jealousy. Dogs often do not do well with change, so if all of a sudden a dog isn't getting 100% of the attention it is used to receiving, it can act out, typically by ploys like barking, jumping or nipping. But this can turn into more destructive behavior like stealing shoes, tearing at the furniture or in extreme cases, aggression, particularly if a couple is getting intimate.

What are ways to help your pet adjust to a new love, and vice versa?

The best way to get the dog to adjust to an additional

APPENDIX 1

presence is for the new person to create a bond with the dog and form their own relationship. Simple things like taking the dog for a walk or playing fetch, tug or catch will not only forge a bond but provides the opportunity for "directed guidance" which promotes respect. Another great method is for the new person to teach a dog a trick. By providing this kind of structure, in a fun and positive way, the dog will soon seek to please and mind both of the partners instead of just one.

Is visiting a trainer helpful, why?

Absolutely, because a qualified trainer will ask a lot of questions to better assess the situation and because they are on the outside looking in, may be able to offer some suggestions that the couple hasn't considered. One thing I run in to a lot is having to re-train dogs that have been taught incorrectly by well-meaning but misguided owners or inexperienced trainers. A good

APPENDIX 1

trainer understands that they're not just training the dog but they're also training the owner. Training can help stop a lot of problematic behavior but it is up to the owner to remain consistent in what they've learned.

A dog's memory isn't like an Etch-A-Sketch where you can just shake it and start from scratch. So regardless if you work with a professional or train your dog on your own it is important to stay consistent, positive and do everything you can to get it right the first time.

What are ways they can bond?

Having fun in an activity with the dog is the best way to bond with a dog that is new (to you). Going for a walk or a hike or even some interactive play is a great way to bond with a dog as long as that play has some boundaries. I'm also a big proponent of being hands-on with a dog so a nice massage or

APPENDIX 1

even just a gentle petting when watching TV can help instill trust and closeness.

What can you do if they just don't get along?

They will! But it may take some time and effort and remember consistency is key. This is where the help of a qualified, positively oriented trainer and behaviorist will be helpful. That way you can avoid the problem getting worse, and it will be much easier to fix if you start right from the beginning.

One thing I strongly recommend avoiding is sequestering the dog when the new person comes over. I am an advocate of teaching dogs early on that it's OK to be alone. By getting a dog accustomed to a crate or dog gate, and having it be a positive experience, many problem behaviors can be curtailed. But if the dog is just put away when the new person drops by then jealousy, anxiety and anger can be created.

APPENDIX 1

What behaviors should you look out for?

If the dog is particularly aggressive to strangers it is best to seek the help of a professional positively based trainer. However, in some cases it just might be a low-level fear that will go away quickly when the dog has a chance to accept and trust the new person. Keeping the dog and new person at a safe and comfortable distance so they can get used to each other will help. Going on walks together, where the dog has a chance to experience the new person as a pleasant addition to fun things they already do can be helpful.

Additionally, for a fearful dog it is much better to ignore the dog until the dog decides it is comfortable and wants the attention of the new person. And if the new person ignores the dog for just a little longer than may seem necessary the end result will typically be the dog wanting to be friends that much more.

APPENDIX 1

This is a better approach than forcing yourself on a fearful dog which may end up creating a more negative outcome.

Do pets feel jealous?

(*See above*). Not only do pets get jealous but as we all know, people get jealous too. I've had people bring me their dogs to "fix" and quickly realized that the dog is fine, it's just responding to its environment. The problem is the new person in the relationship being unwilling to share their partner and actually sabotaging the situation. It's like people getting married when one of them already has children. You either buy in to the whole package and make it a positive situation or you fight it and create problems.

APPENDIX 1

How long should adjustments take?

People who have never had pets are often shocked as to how quickly and strongly bonding can take place when the give and take is there from both the dog and the person. If you're looking for more focused training then strong results typically take hold in 2 to 3 weeks although it may take longer depending on the training methods and goals. Dogs that have serious problems adjusting to new people may take quite a bit longer to come around, conceivably several months, and in rare cases where dogs have deep-rooted and insurmountable fears it may never take place.

APPENDIX 2

INSURANCE ISSUES:

How To Deal With Your Pet Insurance Policy When Separating Or Divorcing

By Embrace Pet Insurance, 1-800-511-9172, embracepetinsurance.com

There are a number of scenarios that can come up in a divorce or separation that involve pets and pet insurance policies.

Scenario 1: You have sole custody of the pets and you have always owned the pet insurance policy yourself.

Check your policy details for the following:

• Who is listed as the insured on the policy?

You can have two or more insureds on a pet insurance policy, all of whom can all make decisions about the policy, including cancellation and billing

APPENDIX 2

decisions. Make sure your policy is limited to the people you want to be making those changes.

• How is the policy paid for and by whom?

Make sure you confirm the billing is your own credit card or bank account as soon as possible. You don't want your ex cancelling the premium payments and lapsing the coverage. Make sure that if the payments come out of a bank account, the account is going to remain active going forward.

• Which addresses are listed on the policy?

Couple of issues here.

• Your premium may change upon a change of address - not much you can do about this but don't be surprised by an unexpected change when your next premium is billed

• You don't want your claim check going to your ex so confirm they are all going to your current location. Even better, have the claim reimbursement

APPENDIX 2

deposited into your own bank account so there's no way for the money to go elsewhere by mistake

• Make sure the email address on record is your current one. You don't want your email going to a defunct address or worse, your ex's.

Scenario 2: You have sole custody of the pets but your spouse owned the pet insurance policy before your split.

If you are taking on the policy from your spouse, you'll have to transfer it into your name as soon as possible. Call the pet insurance company to find out their procedure for transferring the policy as most will allow you to do it. You do not want to have to restart the policy as this might trigger new pre-existing conditions, which you do not want to happen.

If the policy has lapsed for non-payment, ask the pet insurer if the policy can be reinstated without

APPENDIX 2

restarting the policy. If it is just a couple of weeks from lapsing, it's a good bet they'll reinstate your policy as long as you pay the unpaid premium. If it's longer than that and the company says no, plead your case to the underwriter who issued the policy for some leniency. You will still have to pay unpaid premiums if the insurer agrees. Once you have control of the policy, check the policy details in scenario 1.

Scenario 3: You are sharing custody and the finances of the pets. If you are sharing custody of the pets on the policy and want to share the cost of the policy and have the reimbursements go to the appropriate person, this gets tricky. Most pet insurance companies cannot handle multiple bank accounts or addresses for premium payments and claims reimbursement depending on who paid for the vet bill so you will need to coordinate the financials

APPENDIX 2

with your ex. You should include how you are going to do this in your divorce settlement. Note that if you just want to pay for your own policy to cover any vet bills you might have when you have your pets, your spouse does not need to get involved in your policy. It's totally up to you.

Scenario 4: The pets on the policy go to
different homes.

Some insurers have multiple pets on a policy so it becomes complicated when some of the pets stay on the old policy and some go to a new home. The pets that are going to a new home will be split off from the old policy onto a new one, possibly trigger new pre-existing conditions for those pets.

Ask the pet insurer if a special dispensation could be made so that the new policy does not trigger new pre-existing conditions.

APPENDIX 2

Most pet insurers will have no difficulty accommodating this request. Under all the scenarios, if something goes wrong with the policy and you do not get the solution you are looking for from your pet insurer, be sure to write to the insurance company that issued your pet insurance policy for compassionate review. You can often get a positive response if you go right to the source.

APPENDIX 3

PARENTING PLAN FOR_____

Parent A: _____

Parent B: _____

Primary Veterinarian:

_____

_____

_____

EMERGENCY CONTACTS:

Parent A's backup:

_____

_____

_____

Parent B's backup:

_____

_____

APPENDIX 3

Regular Schedule:

Parent A: _____

Parent B: _____

Monday: _____

_____

Tuesday: _____

_____

Wednesday: _____

_____

Thursday: _____

_____

Friday: _____

_____

Saturday: _____

_____

Sunday: _____

APPENDIX 3

Vacation Schedule for Parent A:

Winter Vacation: ____ *weeks in* _____

Spring Vacation: ____ *weeks in* _____

Summer Vacation: ____ *weeks in* _____

Fall Vacation: ____ *weeks in* _____

Vacation Schedule for Parent B:

Winter Vacation: ____ *weeks in* _____

Spring Vacation: ____ *weeks in* _____

Summer Vacation: ____ *weeks in* _____

Fall Vacation: ____ *weeks in* _____

Holiday Schedule

Parents can choose to alternate years by using and "odd" "even" year designation, or they can choose to always have certain holidays.

Parent   A   B

APPENDIX 3

New Years Day _____

_____

Valentine's Day _____

_____

St. Patrick's Day _____

_____

April Fools _____

_____

Easter _____

_____

Memorial Day _____

_____

4th of July _____

_____

Labor Day _____

_____

Halloween _____

APPENDIX 3

Thanksgiving _____

_____

Channukah _____

_____

Christmas Eve _____

_____

Christmas Day _____

_____

New Year's Eve _____

_____

Travel Arrangements

Air Travel: _____

_____

_____

_____

APPENDIX 3

Road Trips:

_____

_____

_____

_____

_____

Doggie Daycare

_____

_____

_____

_____

Boarding

_____

_____

_____

_____

APPENDIX 3

Agreements on food

Regular Food: _____

_____

_____

_____

_____

Treats:

_____

_____

_____

_____

Grooming

_____

_____

_____

_____

APPENDIX 3

Veterinary Treatment

_____

_____

_____

_____

Shared Costs

_____

_____

_____

_____

Moving Away

_____

_____

_____

_____

APPENDIX 3

End of Life Decisions

_____

_____

_____

_____

_____

_____

_____

_____

APPENDIX 4 – RECORDS
MEDICAL RECORDS

Month 01 Date:_____	Month 02 Date:_____
☐ Flea/Tick Med. Weight:_____ ☐ Heartworm Med. ☐ Bath/Groom. ☐ Trim Nails	☐ Flea/Tick Med. Weight:_____ ☐ Heartworm Med. ☐ Bath/Groom. ☐ Trim Nails
Month 03 Date:_____	Month 04 Date:_____
☐ Flea/Tick Med. Weight:_____ ☐ Heartworm Med. ☐ Bath/Groom. ☐ Trim Nails	☐ Flea/Tick Med. Weight:_____ ☐ Heartworm Med. ☐ Bath/Groom. ☐ Trim Nails
Month 05 Date:_____	Month 06 Date:_____
☐ Flea/Tick Med. Weight:_____ ☐ Heartworm Med. ☐ Bath/Groom. ☐ Trim Nails	☐ Flea/Tick Med. Weight:_____ ☐ Heartworm Med. ☐ Bath/Groom. ☐ Trim Nails
Month: Date:_____	Month: Date:_____

☐ Fecal Exam #1
   REMINDER
☐ Heartworm R_x Renewal
☐ Flea/Tick R_x Renewal
	☐ Dental (if needed)
	   REMINDER
	☐ Vaccinations

Feeding Instructions:

_____

_____

_____

_____

APPENDIX 4 – RECORDS
MEDICAL RECORDS

Month 07 Date:_____	Month 08 Date:_____
☐ Flea/Tick Med. Weight:_____	☐ Flea/Tick Med. Weight:_____
☐ Heartworm Med.	☐ Heartworm Med.
☐ Bath/Groom.	☐ Bath/Groom.
☐ Trim Nails	☐ Trim Nails
Month 09 Date:_____	**Month 10** Date:_____
☐ Flea/Tick Med. Weight:_____	☐ Flea/Tick Med. Weight:_____
☐ Heartworm Med.	☐ Heartworm Med.
☐ Bath/Groom.	☐ Bath/Groom.
☐ Trim Nails	☐ Trim Nails
Month 11 Date:_____	**Month 12** Date:_____
☐ Flea/Tick Med. Weight:_____	☐ Flea/Tick Med. Weight:_____
☐ Heartworm Med.	☐ Heartworm Med.
☐ Bath/Groom.	☐ Bath/Groom.
☐ Trim Nails	☐ Trim Nails
Month: Date:_____	**Month:** Date:_____
☐ Fecal Exam #2	☐ Dental (if needed)
REMINDER	REMINDER
☐ Heartworm R_x Renewal	☐ Vaccinations
☐ Flea/Tick R_x Renewal	

Feeding Instructions:

_____

_____

_____

_____

APPENDIX 4 – RECORDS
MEDICAL RECORDS

Pet's Name: _____

Age: _____ Sex ____ Neuter/Spay (Y/N)

Health Condition: _____
Medication: _____

Medication: _____

Medication: _____

Veterinary Visit (last): _____

Vaccinations:

_____   _____

_____   _____

Heartworm Medication: _____
Topical Flea/Tick Med.: _____
Pet Insurance Policy Number: _____
Pet Insurance Company Name: _____
Pet Insurance Claims Dept.: _____

About the Authors

Steven May

Steven May is a pet expert and has been working in the veterinary industry for over 35 years. He lectures on marketing, public relations, communications and brand strategy for the Pet and Veterinary Industries. He is a sought after speaker, and author. May published a lifestyle and practice management publication for Veterinarians named VETZ Magazine.

Steven's blog, *The Daily Growl* (www.DailyGrowlBlog.com) is an internationally respected resource for information about all types of pets and pet care.

Steven has appeared in PEOPLE Magazine, CNN, Reuters, AP News, Los Angeles Times, Chicago Tribune, New York Times, plus over 100 various national and international media newspapers and magazines. Currently May provides expert advice via pet care segments which cover over 25 TV and Radio markets and has been seen on The TODAY Show, ABC Nightly News and other National and local TV media shows.

About the Authors

David T. Pisarra

David Pisarra has been practicing Family Law in California since 1998. He has wide experience in Divorces, Pet Support, Pet Custody, Paternity, Alimony / Spousal Support, and Domestic Violence cases. He has represented both men and women, gay and non-gay people successfully.

He has been a caretaker to three dachshunds, each one stealing more of his heart. As a writer he has written for the Huffington Post, GoodMenProject, Divorce360.com and has a weekly column in the Santa Monica Daily Press. He has three legal guides for men available on Amazon.com and Barnes and Noble.

Our Guides

<u>Current Guides:</u>

What About Wally? Co-Parenting A Pet With Your Ex. Using his life experience as a backdrop, David T. Pisarra explains What a Pet Parenting Plan is, Why you need one, and How to develop one that fits your pet's needs. Steven May uses his 35 years of experience working with pets and the parents who love them, to explain how to work together for the pet's best interests.

<u>Upcoming Guides:</u>

What about Wally? – Estate Planning For Your Best Friend and *Sharing Sally – Co-Parenting for Cats.*

Contact Us for Speaking Engagements:

David@PetLoverzGuides.com

Steven@PetLoverzGuides.com

PETLOVERZGUIDES

CPSIA information can be obtained at www.ICGtesting.com
Printed in the USA
LVOW120931080212

267703LV00008B/57/P